WORLDS END

PAUL SELLAR

Paul studied drama at Bristol University. His plays include: *The Bedsit* (featuring James Ellis) at the Tabard Theatre, transferring to BAC as part of Time Out Critic's Choice season in 1996. Later that year it was produced by The Assembly Rooms for the Edinburgh Festival. Other plays at The Edinburgh Festival include: *Dark is the Night*, a stage adaptation of *The Night Wire* and *The Waxwork* which formed a double bill of mystery and suspense, and a comedy thriller *Cell G159*, that was revived the following year as *The Dead Move Fast* (featuring Sylvester McCoy).

2Graves (featuring Jonathan Moore) premiered at the Pleasance Theatre, Edinburgh 2006 before transferring to London where it re-opened the Arts Theatre. The production featured an original score from Oscar-nominated composer Michael Nyman. *2Graves* marked Paul's West End debut.

Previous commissions have included the National Theatre and his work has been developed at the NT Studio, the Bush Theatre, Soho Theatre (Studio) and The Old Vic. His plays have been produced in Dublin and Chicago.

The Bedsit is published by Faber and Faber and *The Dead Move Fast* and *2Graves* are published by Oberon Books.

He is currently writing a play for BBC radio 3 (The Wire) and an original screenplay for Warp X films.

Paul Sellar

WORLDS END

OBERON BOOKS
LONDON

First published in 2008 by Oberon Books Ltd
521 Caledonian Road, London N7 9RH
Tel: 020 7607 3637 / Fax: 020 7607 3629
e-mail: info@oberonbooks.com
www.oberonbooks.com

A catalogue record for this book is available from the British
Library.

ISBN: 978-1-84002-845-4

Cover design by Dan Steward.

Printed in Great Britain by Antony Rowe Ltd, Chippenham.

For my parents

Characters

BEN

His central characteristic is a paradox. He's
relaxed and edgy. Easygoing and difficult. He
has a sort of wistful cynicism to him though he is
also capable of warmth, charm and romance.

KAT

Kat is a little younger than Ben. Perhaps mid-to
late-twenties. She has finished university and is
now doing a foundation course at Camberwell.

THEA

An old friend of Kat's, they were boarding
at a girls' public school together – Bryanston
in Dorset. She is an estate agent and dresses
fashionably.

JOSH

He is a pleasant, sunny bloke. Well meaning
and generally polite. He possesses a quiet, wry
urbanity which lies beneath the surface.

The action takes place in the living room of a lower ground-floor
flat in Primrose Hill, North West London. It unfolds in real time.
The play is set in the here and now.

Worlds End was first performed at the Pleasance Theatre for the Edinburgh Festival in August 2007. It was presented by Andy Jordan Productions with the following cast:

BEN, Merryn Owen

KAT, Fiona Button

THEA, Monica Bertei

JOSH, Jamie Belman

Director Paul Robinson

Designer Rachael Canning

Music / Sound Richard Hammarton

Lighting Ben Pacey

A revised version of *Worlds End* opened in a new production at the Trafalgar Studios in February 2008. It was presented by Andy Jordan Productions with the following cast:

BEN, Merryn Owen

KAT, Charlotte Lucas

THEA, Monica Bertei

JOSH, Jamie Belman

Director Guy Retallack

Designer Rachael Canning

Music / Sound Richard Hammarton

Lighting Mark Dymock

The play is set in a flat in Primrose Hill, London, NW3. Throughout the action of the play furniture is removed from the room.

BEN is looking out of the window.

BEN: I was right you know. It's still raining.

KAT: Ben? Please?

BEN: Hmm?

KAT: Will you just go? For me?

BEN: What? And miss my own funeral? You must be joking.

KAT: I'm not joking. I'm totally serious. We made an arrangement. You agreed. You promised.

BEN: Promises, promises.

KAT: You swore.

BEN: I lied.

KAT: I'm not happy about this. Not at all.

BEN: I thought you might like to have seen me.

KAT: Hmph.

BEN: It's been a while. I'm sure we've a fair bit to catch up on.

KAT: Ben?

BEN: Kat?

KAT: Ben?

BEN: Kat?

KAT: Please. Just go.

BEN: No.

KAT: What's the matter with you?

BEN: I don't know. I know this. I'm not well. I keep breaking into cold sweats. How do I look?

KAT: Fine.

BEN: Well. I certainly don't feel it. My mind's all over the shop. And I was pissing for England this morning. Couldn't stop. What's wrong with me?

KAT: I don't care.

BEN: No, of course not. Won't be you who's left to pick up the pieces. No, when I finally crack you'll most probably be having your chin surgically removed in a little *pied à terre*. Fulham I should think. I can see it now. Four lines in the *Ham & High*. – 'Book shop employee charged with affray. Terrified staff could only look on as he ran amok through the store assaulting passing shoppers with a tape gun. The post of Stock Room Assistant is currently vacant.'

Pause.

Dear me, it's as cold as a grave in here.

KAT: Why don't you put the heating on?

BEN: You must be joking. I'm not going anywhere near that thing. It's vicious. Look at it. Hissing through its teeth. I wouldn't be surprised if it bites. I just wish the gas board would uproot the fucker and be done with it. Only a matter of time before the whole place goes up with that in the corner.

Beat.

Am I right though? I mean, is he that type? Fulham.

KAT: I'm not sure he's any type.

BEN: Well, he must be yours, though I doubt he's mine. And I'm sure he's doing rather well for himself? You've had your fun with the bohemian types, include me or make me the exception, as is your want... I expect you want a little security now...time to settle down with a suit. I don't suppose you were too fussy. Navy blue, pinstripe, charcoal gray...plenty of choice. Am I warm?

KAT: Sorry I wasn't listening.

BEN: Well you should have been.

KAT: Why?

BEN: Because my curiosity has peaked. And I need answers. I want to know who it is you've left me for.

KAT: I think you should worry about yourself instead of everyone else.

BEN: I am worried about myself. Very worried.

KAT: And so you should be.

BEN: And so I am.

KAT: Too right 'cos it was all wrong you know. You crawling out of bed at two in the afternoon 'cos you'd nothing to do.

BEN: Nothing to be done.

KAT: And your writing?

BEN: Dried up.

KAT: At your age?

BEN: Nothing left to say.

KAT: Don't be ridiculous.

BEN: All been said before.

KAT: Then you need a job.

BEN: I've got a job.

KAT: That's not a job.

BEN: Bloody well is. Unpacking books on a part-time basis confirms my status as an author of integrity. The books I haven't bothered to write being far superior to those others have. My literary ambitions died and I was happy to bury them. You see, I've got it all worked out. If I don't get up till two then that's only four hours to kill. Six being a respectable time to begin my evening. So – four hours of frustration, regret, despair and bitter disappointment but come six and I'm free. Free from the chains of dull reality and after three pints and a shot of gin I'm all the things I could have and should have been and it feels bloody marvellous. Cigarette?

KAT: Told you. I packed them in.

BEN: (*Trying to get his lighter to spark.*) Oh yes. So you said. How long?

KAT: Six weeks.

BEN: Ah. Fresh start on all fronts. Bet seeing me again isn't making it any easier. Do you think he'll come straight from work?

KAT: I'm not happy about this.

BEN: Why, does he not mix well? Is he not genial?

KAT: He's perfectly genial.

BEN: Oh, well. That's good. And don't worry about me. I'm not here to upset anyone. Nor am I torturing myself. Not at all. I'm enjoying myself. I'm really very happy being perfectly miserable and I'm only ever nasty to people when I don't like them. And who knows? He might be my sort. We might just click. Get on famously. What's he like anyway?

KAT: Are you going to leave?

BEN: Well, that depends.

KAT: On what?

BEN: Well… Partly on his name. What is it?

KAT: Does it matter?

BEN: You'd be surprised. I don't mind being ousted after a two year relationship as long as it's not by some loafer-clad, loft-dwelling twat called Miles.

KAT: Well, it's not Miles

BEN: No, then who? Come on, don't keep me guessing. I'm suffering. This is agony. Is there nothing you can tell me?

KAT: I can tell you I like him. That he's good for me and treats me well. He's got a spark about him. He hasn't got time to sit around feeling sorry for himself. He's never put me down or tried to undermine me and he doesn't sulk. At least not for long.

BEN: Sounds like a good 'un.

KAT: Sure is.

BEN: Good.

She goes to bookshelf.

KAT: I'm assuming all these books are mine. I haven't time to go through them. If any of them turn out to be yours I'll send them back.

BEN: Yes. 'If my books dare to roam, box their ears and send them home.' By the time you're through the only thing that'll be left on the shelf is me.

KAT: Don't start feeling sorry for yourself.

BEN: Why not?

KAT: It won't get you anywhere.

BEN: Do you know who you remind me of? The vicar who cut short Spenser's service and lowered the coffin at double speed. Wiped his hands of it quick as he could; just to get in out of the rain. Pissed me off that did. You remember Spenser?

KAT: I remember some old soak in the corner of the pub.

BEN: That old soak had four plays in the West End in the mid fifties. Died penniless and alone. And if I'm being melodramatic then why was I the only one at his funeral?

KAT: Because he wasn't a very nice man.

BEN: He had a big heart, old Spenser. Empty his pockets at the drop of a hat.

KAT: I don't care.

BEN: Nor did that bastard vicar. Running through the gravestones in his long coat with a prayer book over his head. The ignominy of it. He deserved better. And so, come to that, do I. Or don't you agree?

KAT: What?

BEN: You've hardly listened to a bloody word I've said, have you?

KAT: No.

BEN: Why not?

KAT: Heard it all before.

BEN: I don't know why I bother.

KAT: You don't. That's the trouble. You just don't bother anymore. And I'm not happy about being told that I'm walking over your grave. This isn't exactly my idea of a picnic either, you know.

BEN: No?

KAT: No, and that's why I'm getting on with it.

BEN: Getting on with it is one thing. Bulldozing over it is another.

KAT: Ben. Please. Just go.

BEN: Why?

KAT: You know why. Don't make this difficult for me.

BEN: Hmm. I suppose I could take myself off to the Queens. I really shouldn't stay in anyway. Not again. Late night TV for two nights on the spin. No thanks. It's awful. Just when you feel you've hit rock bottom some advert for chat lines comes on to remind you that you're still falling.

Beat.

Where did you meet? Don't tell me it was at that witch's housewarming. And she is a witch even though I know she's a good friend of yours and that she's been there for you throughout etc, etc.

KAT: Well, as it happens…she has.

BEN: How nice.

KAT: Exactly.

BEN: No one was there for me. That's a fact. And it wasn't particularly nice either. Unless, of course you happen to like the idea of living like a complete fucking hermit. Still, I s'pose I'd better get used to it. Perhaps I should buy a big jumper, move to Devon and make it a way of life. And when I do finally pop my clogs I shan't suffer the humiliation of poor old Spenser. No. This man's for burning. Throw me up in flames six feet high and let the ashes scatter as they will.

Beat.

Do you know something?

KAT: What?

BEN: The sickening part of this is that you're still the most beautiful girl I've met. And I'm afraid that doesn't make this any easier and if that sounds shallow then I'm sorry but it's true. You are beautiful.

KAT: To you I am, maybe.

BEN: Yes. To me. You are.

Beat.

Has he told you that too? Because if so then I'm wasting my time.

KAT: You're wasting your time anyway.

BEN: Yes. But has he told you? Does he know? Does he see how beautiful you are?

KAT: Stop it Ben.

BEN: I'd noticed you long before we were introduced. Outside Legends. 'Don't bother,' you said, as you passed me. 'It's not worth it.' But no, I went in, and all night I couldn't get you out of my mind.

KAT: I don't remember

BEN: Well I do. (*Beat.*) Ironic though. Your first words. – 'Don't bother.'

    Beat.

    Have you told him about me?

KAT: Why?

BEN: May have asked.

KAT: About you?

BEN: Yeah.

KAT: I suppose.

BEN: And has he?

KAT: No.

    She wraps a piece of sculpted glass in newspaper.

BEN: I take it you got my letter.

KAT: Yes.

BEN: And ignored it?

KAT: Of course.

BEN: Why?

KAT: We'd split up. I'd moved on.

BEN: Yes. How is Camberwell?

KAT: Great.

BEN: I bet it is.

Beat.

Look at those bare branches. Have you ever seen a leaf on that tree? I haven't. Not since we've been here. All the other trees on the street have leaves. What's the matter with ours?

KAT: You rolling up drunk and pissing on it can't have helped.

BEN: Don't blame me. It was like that when we first moved in.

Beat.

I don't know what to do with myself. I think I'm older than I thought I was and the only person I seem to know anymore is you. (*Ponders again.*) Have you noticed how after a while everyone starts to look more or less the same? Odd, and a little frightening. And then before you know it you've begun to look odd and a little frightening yourself.

Beat.

I s'pose I could dig out my address book. Blow off the cobwebs and make a call or two. But, fuck me, it looks cold out there. What am I going to do? I've forgotten how to pull. I don't stand an earthly.

Beat.

Odd how we never really talked about all this. Don't you think?

KAT: We did. I explained when I first came in but it just didn't get through.

BEN: Didn't make any sense.

KAT: It did to me.

BEN: You always used to say if I sorted myself out.

KAT: That was then and anyway…you never did phone Dr Fisher did you?

Beat.

I'm not saying it's easy but there's no shame in it you know. He did a lot for me.

BEN: Hmm. (*Looks back out window.*) Shit.

KAT: What?

BEN: I've just seen one.

KAT: ?

BEN: A magpie. On the branch.

KAT: Salute it.

BEN: Is that a real thing?

KAT: Yeah.

BEN: Oh – it's all right. There's another one now. Two for joy. (*Beat.*) Good. Do you fancy a quick glass of something? I might have a bottle in the fridge. I think there's some Chablis. You like that one don't you? In fact I think it's yours. You wont mind if I help myself? You want one?

KAT: No. I've got to get on.

BEN: Fine. Never mind. You just get on, then.

KAT: (*As if to say: please don't take it like that.*) Ben?

BEN: No. Really.

KAT: Okay. Okay. I will. Get on.

BEN: Good don't let me stand in your way.

KAT: Don't worry. I won't.

BEN: No. If you're going. Go.

KAT continues to pack stuff up. She's doing a good job. Bubble wrap, scissors, some tea chest type boxes, etc.

You're doing a very professional job. A credit to Camberwell. Of course, it's not just what they've taught you. It has to be in you. And, my God, it is. Those hands can twist life out of a lump of clay in a manner that makes me wince. I can hardly bear to watch.

KAT: I don't know why you do.

BEN: When I see you splashing about with a lump of clay and twisting it and carving it and slapping it into shape, I feel a great amount of empathy with that lump of clay. I'm sure I know just how it feels. There is strength and a grip in those fingers that could rip a heart out and then squash it flat in your bare hands.

KAT: What are you talking about now, dickhead?

BEN: I'm talking about your lack of compassion.

KAT: My what?

BEN: It's not that you're leaving me. It's the efficient professionalism with which you're doing it.

KAT: Yes, well...no point in dragging it out.

BEN: No. Well then just put me out of my misery.

KAT: How do I do that?

BEN: By telling me everything.

KAT: About what?

BEN: I don't know. Everything? His name? Anything. Don't keep me guessing. This is agony. I'm suffering.

KAT: Are you?

BEN: Yes.

KAT: Good.

BEN: Kat?

KAT: I'm glad. I hope you cry yourself to sleep.

BEN: This isn't you?

KAT: Yes it is. It is. This is me. That silly little infatuated girl that you went out with – that wasn't me. Do you know I'm embarrassed when I look back at how much I loved you? What a fool I made of myself. Standing up for you. Letting you walk all over me. I must have looked such a fool. Running after you in floods of tears. Jumping on your car. Begging you not to leave. On my knees. In tears. For you. I must have been mad. Out of my mind. (*She shudders.*) Uggh.

BEN: I think you're being a little hard on yourself.

KAT: I don't care what you think. I've wasted enough time on you already. It's about time you knew what it was like to feel like shit. Might just give you a little dash of humility.

BEN: Kat?

KAT: A tiny dollop of compassion.

BEN: That's not very nice.

KAT: Well, nor were you. Oh – and I'm very happy with my life now. And now I know what it means to be in a real relationship. With a real man. Where I feel happy, comfortable and safe. He dresses well, he's thoughtful and romantic, sexy and he's very good in bed. Oh and his name, since you keep asking, is Josh. Now pass me that basket, will you?

He does so.

Thank you.

BEN: Quite all right. (*Pause.*) Josh? Josh, Josh, Josh. Don't believe I know a Josh.

Beat.

20

Well, as long as you're to be happy. And I'm sure he's doing very well for himself. Earning a crust. Well, it'll make a nice change for you won't it? You'll be able to bask. I can see it now. The pair of you. Basking.

KAT takes down a colourful wall hanging.

I was so happy in that little shop, haggling over that for you. 500 euros in my hand. Looking round. And when my time was up. You'll remember we took turns to mind the luggage, and I'd walked out into the Mediterranean heat and I saw you sitting on our luggage eating a souvlaki. And I thought, my God, you cheeky little thing. You must have nipped off and left our bags to get it and now you're trying to finish it off, gobble up the evidence before I got back. And it was then that I felt my eyes well up because it was then that I knew deep down that I wouldn't love anyone else. At least, not in the same way that I loved you.

KAT: It wasn't a souvlaki. It was a pitta-bread roll. And I bought it from a man with a tray. So you see, it wasn't actually me who you fell in love with, anyway.

BEN: I know a pitta-bread roll from a souvlaki and you were eating a souvlaki.

KAT: Believe what you like.

BEN: I know what I saw.

KAT: I know what I ate.

BEN: There was no man with a tray.

Beat.

And what difference does it make now anyway? It's over and good riddance as far as I'm concerned.

Beat. BEN paces the room.

So how long have you been seeing Josh, then?

KAT: A few weeks.

BEN: That all?

Beat.

Is he at Camberwell, then? This real man of yours?

KAT: No, he's not. He's not at Camberwell. I met him while I was doing some art classes in prison as part of a rehab programme. I was in Maidstone where he was on remand. He'd been bound over for GBH. It was a crime of passion, you see, and he's a big lad and a bit on the rough side, and jealous as hell – but I cream myself watching him fight over me and we argue like mad but then the make-up sex is fucking fantastic. Only downside is he's a little bit possessive and when he heard where I was coming today he punched a hole in the wall the size of frigging crater.

Door bell.

That's the door.

BEN: I know.

KAT exits.

THEA: Hi babe.

KAT: Thea? What are you doing here?

THEA: I thought you wanted help.

KAT: Sure – but I thought you were working late.

THEA: I got someone to cover.

KAT: Oh. Good. Thanks. Listen. There's a problem.

THEA: What?

KAT: Ben.

THEA: Is he here?

THEA enters followed by KAT.

What the fuck are you doing?

BEN: Excuse me?

THEA: Why are you here?

BEN: I wouldn't miss this for the world.

THEA: What?

BEN: I've got the best seat in the house.

THEA: !

BEN: I booked early to avoid disappointment.

THEA: You promised me you'd be out.

BEN: I know. But I'm in. And you knew I would be.

THEA: What are you talking about?

BEN: ?

THEA: Will you just go?

BEN: No.

THEA: You're being an arse. You know that, don't you? (*To KAT.*) You okay?

KAT: Yeah.

THEA: Right. Well – let's get stuck in anyway. I've got to get back soon.

KAT: Appointments?

THEA: Just the one. Grotty little hovel off the Abbey Road. Where shall we start? Bags in the hall?

KAT: Yeah. Or you could start with the landing.

BEN: Yeah. Start with the landing.

THEA: Excuse me.

BEN: Fuck the hall.

THEA: What are you doing here anyway?

BEN: I could ask the same of you.

THEA: What?

BEN: You heard.

Mobile rings. KAT answers it.

KAT: Hello? (*Listens.*) Oh, hi babe. (*Listens.*) What? Didn't you get my – well, I said not to – There's a change of plan. Could you come round later instead?

From now on we hear JOSH as well and, maybe his footsteps as well, from outside.

JOSH: (*Out of view.*) But I'm here.

KAT: (*Into phone.*) What?

JOSH: (*Out of view.*) I'm coming down the steps now.

KAT: Shit. (*Back into phone.*) Josh?

JOSH: I'm at the front door.

KAT: (*Into phone.*) But there's a problem.

JOSH: (*Out of view.*) What?

Doorbell.

(*Out of view.*) That's me.

KAT: (*Into phone.*) I know. Look the thing is...hang on.

KAT exits.

BEN: Oh dear.

THEA: Watch it.

BEN: What a mess.

THEA: Behave.

We hear KAT open the front door and talk with JOSH.

KAT: (*Off stage.*) Sorry Josh. Do you mind? It's just that Ben. He's here.

JOSH: Oh.

KAT: He won't go. Could you come back later this evening?

JOSH: Umm. Well – I'm here now.

KAT: Please. For me.

JOSH: Tell you what. I'll wait in the van.

KAT: Okay. That's a good idea. Wait in the van.

BEN: That's it. Wait in the van.

THEA: (*To* BEN.) Stop it.

JOSH: It's a bit silly me waiting in the van isn't it? We just want to get this lot out. Look let's just all discuss it reasonably.

JOSH enters followed by KAT.

Hi. I take it you're Ben.

BEN: Yes.

JOSH: Right. Now look. I'm sorry. I know this is all a bit tough for you and everything but do you think you could just leave us for about half an hour? Just to get the stuff out?

BEN: For half an hour?

JOSH: Yes.

BEN: Just to get the stuff out?

JOSH: Yes.

BEN: No.

JOSH: It isn't fair on Kat.

BEN: It's not fair on me, either.

THEA: He wants to make it difficult.

JOSH: Come on Ben. Is the age of chivalry dead?

KAT: Ben? Can you leave?

BEN: No.

Pause.

It's my flat.

JOSH: But I thought you were going to be out anyway.

BEN: I thought you were going to wait in the van.

THEA: Josh. Ignore him.

JOSH: (*To* KAT.) There's no point in me waiting out there, is there?

KAT thinks.

I may as well help. Sooner we're done the better.

KAT: Well, now you're here – you can start with the Chaise.

THEA: Come on then.

They pick it up.

KAT: Will you manage the steps?

JOSH: Oh, I should think so.

BEN: If it's made it all the way from Sweden then a few more steps can't hurt.

KAT: Well, just be careful with it all the same.

JOSH: Sure.

They've exited with it.

BEN: I knew an ex-con wasn't really your type. No, he's a good choice. Bit of a catch.

KAT: Will you please just fuck off?

BEN: Not now. It's all too juicy.

KAT: Ben?

BEN: Friend of Jonty and Fi's is he? Part of that set?

KAT: What does it matter?

BEN: I knew you'd play it safe.

KAT: Yes. Well, at least he doesn't scare me.

BEN: Scare you? What are you talking about? Name one time when I ever gave you cause to fear me.

KAT removes a small painting, which reveals a punch hole in the wall.

Oh come on...that was...you weren't even in the room. All right. Two. Give me one other time when you felt scared.

KAT: Scared for you. Not of you. But for you. And I couldn't put myself through it anymore.

THEA: (*Entering.*) You taking the desk, hon?

KAT: Yeah.

THEA: Does it come in half?

KAT: No. But you can fold it. But take the draws out first.

BEN: And have a good snoop in them while you're at it.

THEA: (*Exiting.*) I'll bring down what I can.

BEN: She hasn't been gone that long. She's been out there. Lingering. Like she is now. (*To the wall he thinks THEA'S behind.*) hanging on to our every word. (*Back to KAT.*) And another thing. Please don't ignore me like this all day. You never used to. In fact you're not the same. Do you know I think you're someone else. Who are you? Who are you really? And what have you done to the Kat I first met? What did you do to her?

KAT: It's not what I did to her, Ben.

JOSH: (*Entering.*) Looking a bit clearer in the hall.

KAT: Yeah?

JOSH: Got some of the bagged up stuff out the way. Where's Thea?

BEN: Rifling through my drawers.

JOSH: What?

KAT: She's in the bedroom.

JOSH: Thought I'd shut her in the van for a minute.

BEN: No such luck.

JOSH: Is there a problem?

BEN: I don't know. Is there?

KAT: Is the van full?

JOSH: No, though there's not that much space left.

KAT: Don't worry. A lot of it's for the skip.

BEN: I see. You're having a good clear out as well, are you? Well, why not? Not before time, either. I won't be sorry to see the back of it all, anyway.

THEA: (*Entering. To KAT.*) I've left both bags by the door. I wasn't sure what was for the skip and what was coming.

KAT: Don't worry. I'll sort it. Thanks.

THEA: (*Referring to bean-bag.*) hon, is this coming?

BEN: Of course it's bloody coming. What else would you sit crossed-legged on, swapping lamp-lit views on Tantric sex and Kho Samui?

KAT: It should squeeze in.

THEA throws the bean-bag into the trunk. KAT fits it in then she takes a colourful mask off the wall.

BEN: Oh you're taking that too are you? Good. It's a spooky fucker. Like an Inca Death Mask. Be glad to see the back of it. Might just lift the curse.

KAT: Those DVDs are coming.

JOSH: Right.

BEN: Not all. In fact – some of them are mine. But it's easy to decipher. I'm all *South Park, Six Feet Under* and Nick Drake and Kat's more *Will & Grace, Desperate Housewives* and Lily Allen. You'll suss it.

THEA: And the books?

KAT: Yup. I've boxed them up already. Except the travel guides, babe. Can you pass me those?

THEA is about to get them.

BEN: Excuse me.

KAT: Hmm?

BEN: I've put all my notes in those.

KAT: You said they were touristy.

BEN: Yes, but now that they're battered and full of little drawings I like them.

KAT: Fine.

BEN: Good. Well – that was relatively painless.

KAT: And can you pass me that lamp?

THEA passes the lava lamp to KAT. She puts it on top of the bean-bag. JOSH packs up the CDs into a separate box.

JOSH: Box set of *Lost*?

KAT nods and JOSH packs it. The room is thinning out before BEN's eyes as they continue to remove and pack up items.

BEN: It's like being devoured by a pack of piranha. Be rolled into a pauper's grave or left to die in a ditch if you had your way. I might have to get some sort of a steady job.

I'm tired of being poor. It's boring.

Beat.

Always fancied myself as a regional arts critic. Little cottage in the Cotswolds. File a couple of hundred words and then off to the local for a pint of ale. Knocking off some pretty post grad at the weekends.

KAT: (*Closes trunk and stands.*) Josh?

JOSH takes one end. They cart it out. They've gone. BEN and THEA are alone.

BEN: I don't suppose you're too sorry about all this.

THEA: Eh?

BEN: That she's finally escaping from my evil clutches. I expect you put her up to it in the first place.

THEA: What?

BEN: You heard.

THEA: Don't be silly.

BEN: I'm not. I've got you rumbled.

THEA: Have you?

BEN: I have.

THEA: You were no good for her.

BEN: Oh?

THEA: You're a waster. A dead loss.

BEN: So what?

THEA: So, she's best shot of you.

BEN: Do you know I think you're toxic?

THEA: Oh?

BEN: And brutal too? You'll still be tearing me down long after I've gone. Like an Egyptian Queen stoning the corpse of a Persian rebel.

THEA: I'd be careful if I were you.

BEN: I've tried biting my tongue. Just fills my mouth with blood.

THEA: What do you do all day? Swan about with a notebook, living off Kat?

BEN: I knew you were spiteful, but I had no idea you were unhappy as well.

THEA: It's all talk.

BEN: I've written.

THEA: About what?

BEN: Life.

THEA: It's a front. That's why Kat can't stay with you. There's nothing to hold onto.

BEN: How about you? Could you find something to hold onto?

THEA: Don't make me laugh.

BEN: I don't remember you being in any great hurry to leave the other day.

THEA: I could never end up with you.

BEN: Why not?

THEA: You'd be bad for me. For my soul.

BEN: Your soul? And where's that? No, don't tell me. Marrakech.

THEA: Fifth floor of Harvey Nicks.

BEN: Why aren't I surprised?

THEA: Perhaps you've seen their winter collection.

BEN: The only collection I've seen is that rag-bag of no hopers you marched in and out of your bed.

THEA: Oh?

BEN: Yes. I think you should take the beam out of your own eyes before turning it on anyone else. What happened to the earnestly virginal rasta who vowed you were his first?

THEA: What about him?

BEN: I'd love to have seen your face when his wife kicked down your door. What did she do? Drag him back to Balham by his dreads?

THEA: He lived in Tooting.

BEN: Well, at least he had a fixed address, I s'pose. Not like Giles, in his painfully trendy houseboat and certainly not like Dan. Fancy living in the back of a VW camper.

THEA: At least we were free.

BEN: He was free to piss off all right.

THEA: His band reformed.

BEN: And he left you so fast he was still doing up his flies on his way to Glastonbury.

THEA: And how do you know about that?

BEN: How do you think?

KAT: From Kat?

BEN: I know lots.

KAT: Like what?

BEN: Well – I know you don't hide those desperate little glances half as well as you think you do.

THEA: You think you know it all don't you?

BEN: Not all – but just enough to flit your clit.

She goes to slap him. Enter KAT.

KAT: Is he winding you up?

THEA: He's trying his best.

BEN: It's been effortless.

THEA: He's been working his little socks off.

KAT: He's not the only one.

THEA: You tired, hon?

KAT: Just a bit. It's Josh, though. He's cleared the landings. Working like a Trojan.

BEN: Maybe he's not very comfortable here. I'm sure he's dying to leave. Can hardly blame him for wanting to push on.

Enter JOSH.

JOSH: Sorry. I'm having a little trouble with the Japanese Armoire.

THEA: What's up, hon?

JOSH: I want to get it towards the back of the van.

KAT: Leave it, Josh. It's expensive. I'll have it delivered.

JOSH: Right. Only it's stuck, you see.

KAT: Stuck?

JOSH: In the front door.

THEA: How can it be stuck?

JOSH: It's sort of...wedged.

THEA: Oh, for God's sake. Have you tried turning it on its side?

JOSH: No. And now it's stuck I'm not sure I want to...well, I'm worried it might...

KAT: Can you help Josh with the wardrobe please?

BEN: Me? Oh okay. Anything to hurry this up. (*He picks it up.*) And don't worry. I'll be gentle with it.

BEN exits with JOSH.

THEA: So how's it going with Josh?

KAT: Good. Sure. Early days – as you know but... Yeah.

Beat.

THEA: And how was it? Earlier?

KAT: Ben?

THEA nods.

Difficult. He'd made an effort. And it was so awkward. He wouldn't leave and...I felt guilty. He wanted to be angry with me but he was too pleased to see me. He just couldn't accept that I'd moved on. I tried to explain. That it was to do with me. I kept repeating that; but I wasn't getting through. There was this slightly sad look in his eyes...the same look I saw in them the very first time I saw him. Yes, he was happy to see me and sad at the same time and that was hard. And of course he was angry and I can't blame him.

THEA: ?

KAT: It was a betrayal. He was suffering and I couldn't handle it. So I left and that wasn't fair.

THEA: Well – don't be too hard on yourself hon.

KAT: No, I guess not. And I was very angry with him. Maybe it was a sort of revenge. The way I left... I just lay in bed unable to sleep and I just knew it wasn't right. So I crept about, careful not to wake him, packed a few things, scribbled a note and left. And that wasn't right.

THEA: Well, there's never a right way to leave someone, is there? You just needed some time, that's all.

KAT: Hmm.

THEA: And Josh is great.

Beat.

Come on. Let's just get through this as quick as we can.

BEN returns out of breath.

Dear me. Look at the state of that.

BEN: Yes, well I've let myself go. (*To KAT.*) Yes, as of tomorrow, a new leaf will be turned over. A few sit ups each morning. I'll be a new man.

KAT: Don't make me laugh.

BEN: You'll be laughing on the other side of your face when I've turned this into a six pack. Uphill – yes, but it'll be worth it for the view. (*Enter JOSH.*) Look at Josh. He's been working away since he's got here and yet he's as fresh as a daisy. Not a hair out of place. Could have walked straight off the cover of *GQ.* Mind you, being well turned out goes with the territory.

JOSH: What?

BEN: I expect you have to be well groomed for the city.

JOSH: I expect you do. But I'm not in the city.

BEN: No. It's all new media these days. The big bucks. Or pharmaceuticals. They're the growth areas. Still, fact remains that you do know how to look after yourself. And your shoes.

THEA: Don't listen.

KAT: Josh, he's –

JOSH: I know what he's doing. I'm not stupid.

BEN: Of course not. Stock brokers rarely are.

JOSH: Shall we get on?

THEA: Good idea.

KAT: (*To BEN.*) Don't push it.

BEN: Me?

KAT: Stop it.

BEN: Why? It's harmless. The only reason I'm interested in what people do is because I don't do anything. I have no prospects. This, truth be told, is why she's leaving me. Though she won't admit it. Not even to herself.

KAT: I said stop it Ben.

BEN: Don't be so feeble. It's not you I'm tormenting. It's myself. Nobody wants a struggling author. And who can blame them? Even I'm a little fed up with my own company. I'd rather be drinking left over mulled wine at congenial gatherings in Primrose Hill but the invites haven't been flooding in. Not this year.

THEA: Not very surprising.

BEN: Oh?

THEA: No. Because you're not very nice. And you wallow in nauseating amounts of self pity and people can't be bothered to waste their time on you.

BEN: Of course they can't.

THEA: No, they've far better things to do.

BEN: Wish I had.

KAT: What time's your appointment?

THEA: Eight.

KAT: Are you sure you'll make it? I don't want to land you in it.

THEA: Should be okay. So long as we're through by half past.

JOSH: Should make that.

BEN: Half past? (*Looks at clock.*) Never. There's stuff all over the place.

JOSH: I've cleared the landing. It's just a few bits in the hall, isn't it?

BEN: And in here. And everything you see in here belongs to Kat. The whole lot. From the South American cheese plant to the minimalist Conran clock. Look at it. Dripping with post millenial affectation. Already past its sell-by. (*Beat.*) Have you noticed a theme to this room, yet? A sort of North West Three Bohemia. Where do you live, Josh?

JOSH: Holborn.

BEN: Studio Flat?

JOSH: (*Exiting.*) Loft apartment.

BEN: How very Manhattan. Are you happy there?

JOSH: (*Off.*) No.

BEN: Why not?

JOSH: (*Off.*) It's too small. Kat, are we taking this cardboard box?

KAT: Which one?

JOSH: Tesco.

KAT: Yup. Tesco is for the van and Dixons for the skip.

JOSH: I think this is ASDA.

KAT: Hang on.

She exits leaving BEN and THEA alone.

BEN: Stay with me tonight.

THEA: Why?

BEN: You know why

THEA: So you can hurt someone else?

BEN: All right don't stay. Go enjoy yourself with that heady hedonism to which you've grown so accustomed. London will brace itself. Here she comes...the card carrying fag-hag, beating a path from Westbourne Grove to Old Compton Street where she'll be welcomed into any number of little gay paradises scattered throughout Soho. And there you can camp it up with all the pretty people from Glamour Incorporated while your man for the night is left, clockwatching by the door, holding your coat and looking depressed and depressing and hairy and flat-footed and male. Don't you worry I've seen it.

THEA: You're pathetic aren't you?

BEN: Yes, I am.

THEA: But you really are pathetic.

BEN: Oh, exceptionally.

THEA: Stop blowing out everyone else's candle.

BEN: Why would I be doing that?

THEA: To make yours burn brighter.

BEN: The only candle I'd bother blowing out is yours.

THEA: I wouldn't waste your breath.

Beat.

BEN: I think you should stay with me tonight...

THEA: Why would I want to do that?

BEN: Because I think you'd like it. We could sleep head to toe. I'm feeling kinky. Does it offend you that I find you sexually attractive?

THEA: A little.

BEN: Have you always despised me?

THEA: Always.

BEN: Why?

THEA: Because you're hateful and abusive.

BEN: In what way?

THEA: In every way. Kat hasn't been happy for a long time.

BEN: Nor have I. Speaking of heartache have you heard from Ricardo?

THEA: No.

BEN: Have you taken down his hammock, yet?

THEA: No. He took it down himself.

BEN: When most people go abroad they content themselves with a few snaps, a straw camel and a carton of duty free; but you have to go one step further and bring back a Bolivian drummer.

THEA: He was an extraordinary fuck.

BEN: Didn't the neighbours find it odd that he slept outdoors.

THEA: I've no idea. Why don't you ask them?

BEN: In her *naïveté* Kat was worried for you.

Beat.

Yes. She was. She thought your Bolivian beau was using you. Can you believe that? I imagine she thought he was after welfare or citizenship or something but no...it was plain as day that it was he who was being used. The poor bastard thought you loved him. I tried to tell him that he was just in vogue. A West London fashion accessory. The poor sod was sobbing buckets on our doorstep. Do you enjoy messing people about, you thoughtless cow?

THEA: Fuck you.

39

BEN: It's the stunning snobbery of you that I can't abide. That small-minded naffness. Tell me. When you sweat, is it Evian or Perrier?

THEA: Here's a little proverb. And one you ought to know. 'Horses sweat. Men perspire. And women merely glow'.

BEN: I'd like to see you glow.

THEA: Oh?

BEN: Yes, I think we could work up quite a sweat between us.

THEA: You think so.

BEN: Well, I'd like to give it a go.

THEA: You would, would you?

BEN: Yes I would. Stay.

THEA: Why? So you can fuck me all night and then once more in the morning?

BEN: Yes. And then who knows where from there…

Enter JOSH. Silence. He's all but ignored.

JOSH: Sorry.

THEA: What?

JOSH: Have I interrupted something?

THEA: No. No – it's fine.

She smiles.

How's it going?

JOSH: Not bad. Ploughing through.

THEA: Glad to hear it.

THEA picks up a plant and exits. JOSH is just about to exit with a mirror.

BEN: Where did you meet Kat?

JOSH: What?

BEN: I asked where you met. Don't tell me. I've got it. Salad bar at the ICA. Kat has this friend, you see, who, if the blurb is to be believed, is at the forefront of contemporary dance. He prances about naked with a block of ice. His wife left him a few years ago which I think explains rather more than the programme notes. Cigarette?

JOSH: I don't smoke.

BEN: (*Trying to spark up.*) No? Good for you. What were you doing at the ICA. You don't strike me as a connoisseur of performance art. I expect you just popped in for the café. The risotto is very popular with the young BBC executives.

JOSH: I wouldn't know.

BEN: Of course. I keep forgetting you're in the city.

Beat. BEN looks round.

This room is starting to resemble the way it looked when we first moved in. A while ago now. We were so excited... I can't tell you. Brimming with hope and life and youth. Sad really. To remember it. I had used Kat's trunk as a sort of make shift desk. And put my laptop on it. And the plan was to crack the novel. And Kat had dreams of selling her paintings and she'd had a few up in a café where she worked shifts. We had it sussed. I don't know what went wrong. I spent the advance, maybe drank too much, took it all for granted I guess...oh and I was blocked. Writer's block. Laptop went back in the cupboard where it's been ever since. Instead of me and Kat against the world it became us against each other. We fought over everything. Like a couple of alley cats. She was so disappointed.

Enter THEA.

Ah, there you are. Thought you'd still be snooping about in my desk.

THEA: What have you got to hide?

BEN: Nothing. Kat is wonderful but her friends less so, in my opinion, and of course none of them thought I was good enough for her. Have you met them? They've reconstructed themselves. It's all fair trade coffee, iPods and Buddhist priests on speed dial. But underneath they're the same old selfish hags. These aggressively metrosexual *Tatler*-literate harpies. And their men? You can find them sporting Gucci cufflinks, in Canary Wharf bars. Cash junkies desperate for their next fix and complaining of the hole in their soul. That's the life you can expect my friend and you're welcome to it.

Beat.

In fact let me shake your hand. You've saved me from all that.

Silence.

JOSH: You really do push it, don't you?

BEN: And yet you ride it like a wave.

JOSH: Is that so?

BEN: Well yes. Nothing gets through. You're solid, Josh. Harder it's thrown in; faster it comes back. That's because somewhere in your soul, at the core of your being, you have solace.

JOSH: Solace?

BEN: A secret garden where you can go and close the gate behind you. I envy you that. The tranquillity of it. Me? I have no peace.

JOSH: You're the one making all the noise.

BEN: But only because I have no peace.

Beat.

Maybe that's where it went wrong for me with Kat. She sort of lost faith. And then once the sex goes. Well...there's not much left.

Beat.

JOSH: Amazing.

BEN: Hmm?

JOSH: And yet you just don't see it.

BEN: See what?

JOSH: You've no idea have you?

BEN: What?

JOSH: Never mind.

BEN: What are you talking about?

JOSH: If you could see yourself as others do...

BEN: That's true for everyone.

JOSH: But you just don't see yourself, do you?

BEN: ...

JOSH: You bang on about writer's block and cracking the novel. You're living in a dream world. Kat's mentioned where you get your money from. You scrounge off your parents and call yourself a writer. Maybe you are, I don't know. I don't care.

BEN: Hmm.

JOSH: But I do care about Kat. And well – from what I've heard – I think you owe her a bit of a break. No?

BEN: The way I behaved?

JOSH: Yes.

BEN: I'd take all that with a pinch of salt.

JOSH: Oh, would you?

BEN: Yes. Two sides to every story.

JOSH: Look. In a sense it's none of my business. And I'm not going to get drawn in or wound up by you. I know what you're trying to do but it won't work. You're not my problem. I don't mean that in a bad way – but – I just don't care. Now all I ask of you is that you leave Kat alone. I don't know what sort of a hold it is that you think you have over her but she's clearly moved on now. Clearly. And I like her. And we're just getting to know each other and I think you should just accept that. And respect it. Okay?

No response.

Good. That's all.

Enter THEA and KAT.

Is that the landing done?

KAT: Yeah.

JOSH: Good.

THEA: Just this lot in here really.

They continue to empty the room further. KAT exits. BEN looks round then exits as well. JOSH and THEA are alone.

Well?

JOSH: What? Oh. Yes. I had a little chat. I didn't want to be too hard on him. He's not in a very good way, is he? I think I made my point though. Hope it sunk in. Hard to tell. He's a certain type isn't he?

THEA: He was very good for her at the beginning. She was quite smitten. And he was quite different then...they both were.

JOSH: Really. How?

Enter KAT. She may have overheard THEA. But makes nothing much of it.

KAT: Well, that's the hallway cleared.

THEA: Great.

JOSH: And we're just about done in here aren't we?

KAT: Yeah. Pretty much.

BEN enters holding a coat.

BEN: Who packed this up?

JOSH: Oh. Sorry. I didn't know it was yours.

BEN: It's not. It's Spenser's.

He looks around. A long silence.

You really have stripped this place, haven't you?

KAT: We're getting there.

BEN: Stripped it to the bone.

KAT: Just need to get this lot out.

JOSH: (*To KAT.*) And then we're through, are we?

BEN: It's going to look like an Al Qaeda cell by the time you're through. Which I hope is very soon as, need I remind you, it is my flat and I want to watch TV so all I want is for you all to piss off and leave me alone.

KAT: (*Exiting.*) Going as fast as we can.

BEN: Not fast enough.

JOSH: Well if you'd just let us get on.

BEN: Oh it's my fault now is it?

JOSH: Yes.

BEN: I'm holding you up?

45

JOSH: Yes. That's right you are.

BEN: Rubbish. (*Referring to THEA.*) She's in no hurry to leave.

THEA: What do you mean by that?

BEN: What do you think I mean?

JOSH: (*To THEA.*) Don't worry about it.

BEN: But it is a worry.

JOSH: I was talking to her.

BEN: So was I.

THEA: What do you mean by no rush?

BEN: That's the 64,000 dollar question

THEA: What?

BEN: You heard.

THEA: What are you talking about?

BEN: You're not just here to move boxes.

THEA: I'm here for Kat.

BEN: Course you are.

JOSH: Hey.

BEN: Stay out of it.

JOSH: I'm not going to stand here and watch this.

BEN: Well sit down then – or better still – piss off.

JOSH: Look –

BEN: This is nothing to do with you.

JOSH: …

BEN: It's to do with her. And me.

THEA: Don't flatter yourself.

JOSH: Who do you think you are?

BEN: Stay out of this.

Beat. He turns back on to THEA.

I can see what you want. It's in your eyes. You're like a little well-dressed vulture circling the corpse of my relationship –

THEA: You arrogant bastard.

BEN: Interesting to see that you're not denying it.

THEA: I'm not listening.

BEN: That's the trouble.

But THEA is now very softly chanting a Buddhist mantra to help keep herself calm.

Oh this is very good this is. Three months in Tibet and she thinks she's the Dali fucking Lama – it's not real. Incense is via Chanel. Hipsters from Calvin Klein – she wouldn't put her fingers in the earth – it would ruin her manicure.

JOSH: I'm warning you.

BEN: And I'm warning you Josh. This is the world you'll be moving in. Her affectation typifies it. Beneath the pseudo-hippy façade is a selfish cold fish who looks down her materialistic nose at you unless you happen to have wealth or influence or both. Don't fall for the mask of conscience. It's all me, me, me, me, me in their stifling little world.

KAT: (*Having just entered.*) What the fuck are you talking about?

BEN: Spenser had the measure of you lot.

THEA: Who the hell is this Spenser?

JOSH: I wouldn't even get involved. You'll encourage him.

BEN: I'll tell you who Spenser is. Or was. He was a real fucking person. A human being with beating heart. He

47

cared about things and believe it or not, about people too...yes, strange isn't it? This day and age... But he gave a fuck...he could see beyond his own navel. Unlike us he didn't live in a bubble, a goldfish bowl, totally unaffected by the outside world. He got stuck in. Did things. Changed things.

KAT: Why are you being so difficult?

BEN: I see. It's okay for you to traipse about in my flat all day but I'm the one being difficult.

KAT: Well what do you think?

BEN: Well what do you think I think?

KAT: You know what I think.

BEN: As it happens I don't. As it happens I never do. A word of warning Josh. A note of caution. A little pearl. Never try to second-guess Kat. She'll trip you up every time. Her mind is like a disused gold mine. It lures men to their deaths. You have to break your way in at the dead of night and shuffle through the dark with a pick axe and a torch creeping about in the depths of her psyche. Desperate for the loot but fearful of incurring the wrath of some ancient curse and here's the joke – here's the funny part – you'll never find what it is you were looking for because it was never there in the first place – she's a hoax – a fucking hoax.

JOSH: Okay.

BEN: What?

JOSH: Enough.

BEN: What?

JOSH: You've had your say.

BEN: What do you know? – it's not your world that's falling apart – easy for you to judge me – and what about you? Or are you some sort of a saint?

JOSH: I'm starting to see what Kat meant about you now.

BEN: What?

JOSH: I said –

BEN: Not you. You.

KAT: Me?

BEN: Yes. You. What have you been saying anyway?

KAT: Me? Nothing.

BEN: Never knew you had such a big mouth?

THEA: Look who's talking.

BEN: Sorry – I thought you were in Kathmandu.

THEA: I wish.

JOSH: Lay off her.

BEN: Oh so now you're the White Knight?

JOSH: A fraud and a bully.

BEN: I don't care what you think. I couldn't care less about
any of you – I just want you all out of my flat – (*To KAT.*)
and all I wanted from you – all I wanted, if it's not too
much to ask, was some sort of explanation! You don't just
leave someone like that! You don't just walk out without
so much as a word! I didn't know where you were or
anything! I was confused! Was it something I said? Had
you died? What? And not one call! Not even a text! Not
even so much as a fucking text! And I'm sorry if this is
upsetting you but I don't want you back, I don't even want
an apology – just some sort of an –

*But JOSH has punched BEN who rocks back. BEN touches his nose
it's bleeding.*

BEN: What a mess.

JOSH: …

BEN: What a fucking mess.

JOSH: Fuck's sake – this is who you went out with? What the hell does that say about you?

KAT storms off.

Kat? Sorry – I didn't mean to – Fuck!

JOSH turns to THEA.

I want to get the hell out of here. Just need to load up this chest and then we're done are we?

THEA nods.

Good. I'll put it in the van now.

JOSH exits. THEA crosses to BEN.

THEA: You fucking idiot Ben.

BEN: Ow. Sorry.

THEA: Hold still.

BEN: Is it broken?

THEA: Don't think so.

BEN: …

THEA: Tilt your head back. That's better.

BEN: Hmm.

THEA: Okay?

BEN: Yeah. I'll live.

KAT comes back in with some first aid – a damp cloth and maybe some scissors and is a little put out to see THEA tending to him.

THEA: Hey babe. It's okay. I've got it.

KAT: I'll do it.

THEA: I've got it. It's nearly stopped.

Enter JOSH.

JOSH: Right. Job done.

Beat.

Are we all set?

Pause.

KAT: Josh, could you give Thea a lift to the tube please. She'll be late for her appointment?

JOSH: But the van's full. There's nowhere for her to sit.

THEA: It's all right hon. The office are covering for me anyway. You go. It's fine.

KAT: Josh, could you give Thea a lift to the tube please? She'll be late for her appointment.

JOSH: What now?

No reply.

Okay.

Beat. BEN stands and takes the tissue off THEA and he dabs at his own nose.

JOSH: (*To KAT.*) Five minutes yeah?

KAT: I promise.

JOSH: Tops. They'll be nowhere to park and I can't block up the mews.

KAT: I'll be outside. Don't worry.

JOSH: Okay. (*To THEA.*) Come on, I'll shove the stuff off the seat. You can sit on the clock.

THEA: Ben? Ben?

There is no response.

Well – fuck you then.

She strops off in a hurry followed by JOSH. BEN and KAT are alone.

A silence.

BEN: So, this is it, then. Our last dance.

Silence.

You didn't really expect me to leave the key in a plant pot, did you?

KAT: I think it would have been easier.

BEN: But I wanted to be here when you came.

KAT: So you could humiliate me?

BEN: So I could find out why you left.

KAT: I left 'cos I couldn't stay. I couldn't.

BEN: But we were happy.

KAT: We weren't. I wasn't. And nor were you.

Silence.

And you're still not doing anything about it, are you? You're just festering...in the backroom...of a book shop.

BEN: That job's all I've got. It passes the time...it's peaceful. I open boxes and I think of...you. I'm always thinking of you. This morning I dreamt I was in this small garden. I'm not sure where but it felt like home. I heard your voice and I looked round but you weren't there. And then I woke up.

KAT: I have dreams, too.

Beat.

If only you'd have trusted me. It could have been so different.

BEN: Not a day has gone by when I've not thought about you.

KAT: Makes a change.

BEN: Don't. Please. I'm feeling fragile now. So...handle with care.

KAT: You have to handle this one yourself.

BEN: You're really going then, aren't you?

KAT: Yeah. And you knew I was.

BEN: I didn't. I didn't. I thought you might stay.

KAT: Well, I'm not.

BEN: It's been awful. Stuck down in here. Staring at the phone. Willing it to ring. Pacing about, crying, blowing my nose. Making strange yelps when the memories were too much. I never went out. If a bulb blew, I lit a candle.

KAT: Couldn't face the world.

BEN: Not without you.

KAT: You shouldn't have sat here alone. You should have gone out. Met people.

BEN: If staying in was bad, going out was worse. Pubs were a nightmare. I always sat facing the door. My heart leapt every time it opened. I kept thinking I saw you all over the place. Someone who'd smile like you or hold their cigarette in a certain way. And that would just bring it all back.

Beat.

I've been going mad in here. You sneaked off without a word. You just left... I woke up and you were gone.

KAT: I'm sorry. That was wrong. I should have said something.

BEN: Nobody said anything. Your parents wouldn't let on. Your friends clammed up. I couldn't stop wondering where you were or why you left.

KAT: I needed time.

BEN: Know what kept me going? Knowing you'd have to come back for your stuff. That's what kept me going. Took me ages to find the note. It must have slid under the fridge. But even when I dug it out I was none the wiser. You may as well have written it in Japanese. 'You'll always be with me, somehow.' What does that mean? What does that actually mean?

KAT: It means I didn't want to go.

BEN: Then why did you?

KAT: I had to. We were bad for each other. Trashing ourselves. Dragging one another down.

BEN: Not always.

KAT: I felt so low by the end and unattractive...no confidence...at all.

BEN: Why?

KAT: Because that's how I was made to feel. You'd bang on at me when in and ignore me when out and suspicious, you became so sodding suspicious. Turning me against everyone...criticising everything...no one used to come over.

BEN: They did.

KAT: They didn't.

BEN: Oh come on Kat. I was difficult I know.

KAT: Difficult?

BEN: But only at the end. There were good times too. And I miss them. And you. I was so content with you. And so proud and...all the... I miss the little things. Those little walks, browsing about, looking round, feeling your hand grab mine whenever you wanted to cross the road. Meeting you outside the Steels or inside the Queens. Late nights at the Marathon bar. (*He laughs.*) You choking on that falafel.

KAT: The panic.

BEN: And when we both fell asleep on the phone. Neither of us wanting to hang up.

KAT: I never wanted to hang up.

BEN: And the South of France.

KAT: Walking along the Croisette.

BEN: Swimming at night.

KAT: The full-moon parties.

BEN: Driving through the mountains.

KAT: Those twisting roads. They were scary.

BEN: They were fun.

KAT: Fun if you're driving. Try sitting in the passenger seat.

BEN laughs at the memory of her fear.

BEN: There were so many things…so many little things which – we were happy. Yes, we were…and we just let it slip through our… Where did it go? Where did all that go?

KAT: …

BEN: Where does all that go?

KAT: I don't know.

Beat.

You have no idea how much you hurt me.

BEN: I do.

KAT: No. You don't.

BEN: Yes, I do. I do. And that's why I want to make it up to you.

KAT: Then let me go this time. It's too late for anything else.

Beat. BEN looks out the window. He sees a magpie.

BEN: Oh no. (*Then luckily he thinks he see's another.*) Oh – there's another. Two. That's okay. Do you know why one magpie is for sorrow?

KAT: No.

BEN: No, nor did I. But I heard it on the radio. It's because they mate for life. So if you just see one...it's lost its partner. Sad isn't it?

KAT: Hmm.

Beat.

If only you'd trusted me. If only you'd have...believed in me. Why wouldn't you?

Beat.

BEN: I didn't think I was good enough for you.

Beat.

KAT: I never wanted anyone else.

BEN: Didn't think you'd stay, though. And you didn't, did you?

KAT: You made it impossible for me to. And you said things. Just to hurt me.

BEN: I know. I'm sorry.

KAT: But why say them?

BEN: We were drifting apart. And you wouldn't talk.

KAT: What was there to say?

BEN: I don't know. I was losing you and I was scared.

KAT: Me, too.

She leaves with the last box and puts it in the hall. Comes back in.

I'm off.

BEN: Just like that.

KAT: Yes.

BEN: I can't live without you.

KAT: You'll have to.

She puts on her overcoat.

I don't know what else to say.

BEN: I was a mess, Bambs. I'd gone to pot. This place was a pigsty. But I got up this morning with a spring in my step. Found some bin liners. Cleared the whole place up. All because you were coming round.

KAT: …

BEN: And when I'd done the flat I started on myself. Took a shower and went down to the shops with a real sense of anticipation. It was a crisp day. The sky was white. The leaves crunched under my feet and the air was as sharp as freshly cut apples. And a pretty pram-pushing Spanish *au pair* smiled at me. She may even have winked. I'm not sure, the mind plays tricks, but she definitely smiled. And I smiled back. And I felt good. And in the shop I was so happy that I was sad about it. And I was crying so much that I couldn't face the cashier. So I had to stand with my back to the tills. Sniffling in front of a selection of yoghurts and clotted creams and I thought – but I'm happy. Why am I standing here, with a shopping basket, in tears? And I must have looked a sight. Sobbing at half ten on a Thursday morning, with a pack of razors, a can of air freshener and a card with a hedgehog saying 'I miss you' on it. And all I'm saying really is that… I love you, Kat. I love you with every last drop of love in me. Don't go.

We hear a van hooting outside.

KAT: That's Josh.

BEN: I know.

Beat.

Don't go.

KAT: Don't do this.

BEN: Stay.

KAT: Why?

BEN: I want to make you happy.

KAT: Then let me go.

BEN: I wouldn't leave you.

Beat.

And I am taking steps, you know. I am taking steps.

KAT goes to leave. BEN'S revelation stops her.

I did phone Dr Fisher by the way.

This gets her attention.

KAT: ?

BEN: I called him.

KAT: Why didn't you tell me earlier, when I asked?

BEN: I was going to but...it's part of the thing – you're not supposed to talk about it at first. But I did phone and make an appointment. A quiet little, tree lined, street overlooking the canal. Inside it's all cream walls and wood. Very calm.

KAT: Did you see him? Dr. Fisher?

BEN: No. I saw a jolly Californian in his fifties, a colleague of his I suppose...but the point is, the point is that things come out you see, things come out.

KAT: What things?

BEN: Just things, but I'm going to find a way of...and that's why I was looking forward to seeing you again. To show you how much I was going to change. And to tell you how much I'm going to improve everything for us by taking steps; because I love you. And I know that now. And now that I know that. We'll change things.

KAT: Why didn't you do all this sooner?

BEN: I don't know.

KAT: It's too late, now.

BEN: But I'm taking steps. I know that we can't go on like this. You deserve so much. So much. And, I've learnt my lesson and I'm doing other things so that I can be there for you. Properly.

KAT: What other things?

The van hoots again. Beat. He has no answer, or at least he doesn't answer. Perhaps he's sobbing. Then he just stands there and cries. Cries and cries and cries.

What other things? What other things?

Beat. She looks on. He can't speak. He's still crying. She watches, tranxfixed and melting further.

You had so much going for you. And you just threw it away.

Beat.

I loved you. I loved you more than you'll ever know. Maybe too much. But I was there. I was the one who was there for you Ben.

Beat.

If you'd just got on with it. Done things.

BEN: (*He manages to stop crying just long enough to speak.*) I want the Bambina I knew to walk through that door so that I can hold her close and make everything go away. Do you see?

Silence.

KAT: I'm still in love with you, Ben.

Silence.

But I can't possibly stay.

BEN: You can.

KAT: No, I can't.

BEN: You can. I love you.

They hug and/or kiss.

KAT: And you'd really change?

BEN: Yes. We'll wipe the slate clean. I'm glad they took all your stuff out. We don't need all that baggage.

KAT: A fresh start.

BEN: And we'd move; and I'd get a new job. I've got to make my own way and...I will. From today. And learn to trust... and just... I've been playing for too long. Now I want to do things. Make things happen. And I will.

KAT: And you'd get that glint in your eye again.

BEN: Yes. All I've got to do is...grow up. That's all. And I can do that. I've done it. Today. Well, not earlier...but now. In this moment. I've grown up. No good me blaming everyone else for things that are my fault. All I want now is for us to...get on with it all.

Beat.

And with you...the most beautiful...clever...playful.... spry...impish...kind...strong...loving... sexy...enchanting... captivating...magical girl that I've ever met...together... with the right attitude...we could do anything...we could go anywhere...and we could make it all happen...anything at all...and it would be wonderful.

Beat. Van horn beeps again. She pulls away.

KAT: I'm sorry, baby. I really wish I could.

BEN: You can, though.

Silence. She shakes her head. She moves to the doorway. There is a further silence.

If you happen to see the Kat who you used to be...the one who came with me to France, and sat next to me on the night train, hand in hand, or the Kat who jumped in the fountain in the square... If you see that Kat do you think –?

KAT: I don't think I'll see her.

BEN: But if you do. If you happen to come across her, do you think you could let her know that I'm sorry, and that I've turned over a new leaf, and that I'm sorry for hurting her, and for letting her down. So sorry. Will you tell her?

KAT: If I see her.

BEN: Yes. If you see her. Please let her know.

Beat.

KAT: Bye, Ben.

BEN: Bye, Bambina.

She leaves. The door slams. We'd forgotten how loud it is. BEN watches her go long after she's gone. He shivers, then grabs Spenser's coat and puts it on for warmth. He puts a cigarette in his mouth. Tries to light it but he still can't get his lighter to work. He gives up on this task. He sits very still for a few moments. Taking in the empty room, perhaps, maybe he reaches into the coat pockets and discovers a pen, Spenser's pen, he could look at it and maybe try it out and then leave it by a notebook, as the lights slowly fade...some music covers the blackout...

The End